Unruly Tree

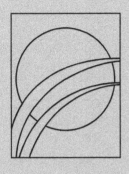

MARY BURRITT CHRISTIANSEN POETRY SERIES

Hilda Raz, Series Editor

The Mary Burritt Christiansen Poetry Series publishes two to four books a year that engage and give voice to the realities of living, working, and experiencing the West and the Border as places and as metaphors. The purpose of the series is to expand access to, and the audience for, quality poetry, both single volumes and anthologies, that can be used for general reading as well as in classrooms.

Also available in the Mary Burritt Christiansen Poetry Series:

For additional titles in the Mary Burritt Christiansen Poetry Series, please visit unmpress.com.

LESLIE ULLMAN

Unruly Tree

poems

UNIVERSITY OF NEW MEXICO PRESS
ALBUQUERQUE

ISBN 978-0-8263-6670-2 (paper)
ISBN 978-0-8263-6671-9 (ePub)

Library of Congress Control Number:
2024939549

Founded in 1889, the University of New
Mexico sits on the traditional homelands of the
Pueblo of Sandia. The original peoples of New
Mexico—Pueblo, Navajo, and Apache—since
time immemorial have deep connections to the
land and have made significant contributions
to the broader community statewide. We honor
the land itself and those who remain stewards
of this land throughout the generations and also
acknowledge our committed relationship to
Indigenous peoples. We gratefully recognize our
history.

Cover illustration: *Metamorphosis* by Dottie
Moore image courtesey of Dottie Moore.
Designed by Isaac Morris
Composed in Didot and Elmhurst

My thanks to Brian Eno and Peter Schmidt
for the nourishment their quirky enterprise
continues to provide.

For the person who follows with trust and forgiveness what occurs to him, the world remains always ready and deep, an inexhaustible environment with the combined vividness of an actuality and flexibility of a dream.

—WILLIAM STAFFORD

Contents

PART II. LEFT-HAND TIME

PART III. BACK-BEAT TIME

Preface

In 1975 composer Brian Eno and artist Peter Schmidt created a list of 110 strategies which they produced as a deck of cards called Oblique Strategies. The deck includes one strategy per card, which is drawn by an artist or composer wishing to be jolted out of a rut and into action. The project arose from the discovery that they approached their art in remarkably similar ways. For Eno, who survives Schmidt and has continued to give interviews on the subject as well as compose a significant body of innovative ambient music, the Strategies evolved from situations of "panic" in which he felt creatively stuck in the middle of limited and expensive studio time. These situations, he recalled, "tended to make me quickly forget that there were . . . tangential ways of attacking a problem that were in many senses more interesting than the direct head-on approach." The Strategies were designed to encourage lateral thinking— to help artists break through barriers and take themselves by surprise.

I was introduced to Oblique Strategies a few years ago when a student in the MFA program at Vermont College of the Fine Arts, where I teach, included them in a handout for her lecture on lists. The clipped, inverted grammar of most of the phrases read like literal translations from another language, reflecting syntax constructed from patterns of thought foreign to me. Although I knew otherwise, I chose to embrace this impression: that the Strategies were half-digested, incomplete fragments whose linguistic origins were so distant as to provide me plenty of room for inventions of my own. In effect, I fell right in with what

Eno and Schmidt intended—engagement with the mystifying challenge of each utterance. I decided to try using all 110 of them as titles and catalysts to poems, each time waiting out a period of resistance and sometimes outright paralysis until something broke through. Ultimately I felt refreshed and free—to play, to write duds—and often I found myself exploring the literary, visual, and musical arts from angles that had never occurred to me before.

The Strategies prompted me to revisit loved paintings and research the painters themselves; to attend concerts where I not only absorbed the music but studied the gestures and facial expressions of the performers; to listen more deeply to jazz, electronic, and popular music; and to observe my own experiences as maker of poems through a new lens. Sometimes I found myself treating the blank page as a musical score in which to manipulate margins and white space in ways new to my ear; in the process I came to experience language as a more malleable and more rhythmic medium than I had before. After all this play and exploration, I was sorry when after four years I got to the last of the Strategies, but I have retained something of the holographic and ever-shifting lens they offered.

Then I spent months revising and culling, with feedback from others, and trying different ways to order the poems. Not all of my 110 experiments were keepers, and I didn't expect them to be. I also felt that to include all of the poems and create a book of over one hundred pages would result in white noise that would keep readers from fully engaging with each poem. This last, hardest part of the work took place during the COVID-19 pandemic and a proliferation of other disasters—mass shootings, police violence, infractions against Americans of color, and repeated attempts to undermine this country's democracy—which remain in the headlines today.

I hope these poems offer, at least by suggestion, some reminder of that most interior and resilient of freedoms—the impulse to fully inhabit and bear witness to an inviolable inner life, an impulse that has persisted in humans throughout history even when shrouded, misunderstood, or denied by circumstance.

Just carry on

Halfway through the grid work of Oblique

I'm wondering how long my visa will last;
if I can grope my way through the next

fifty-five barricades and their slender gaps, fling myself

over each cliff, drift, and sustain
each silence, all quirk
and thermal, no gauges speaking back to me.

I want every hill

and the sound of my breath pushing
metaphor into the dark—

that kind of listening.

Can I stay with the dig, the dirt,
the onslaughts of draught, along with
all this ragweed and thistle?

If the vein runs out, I still want the mine.

I want to cull the best fruit
from an unruly tree.

I want the entire tree.

part I

FLOATING TIME

Listen in total darkness or in a very large room, very quietly

Come first the words you've always
reached for, well-thumbed
thoughts, and your imprimatur

of anxieties; come next the blankness
you shrink from, unpeopled, no signs
to play back the one language you know;

come surrender; come drift,
the need to speak a memory
from the life you've left behind;

come the music of your breath,
hushed notes, a libretto you follow
without words, a face

whose features take shape, melt
and renew themselves from archetypes
rising in your wakened eye;

come dreamed flint, its spark tongue
the song that writes
itself, yours / not yours,

not known to anyone
but you—you may
forget this.

Go slowly all the way around the outside

Outside is one child hidden inside
a neighbor's bushes while the others
are called in from tag and tetherball,
and streetlights whose beams can't penetrate
the rain-scented leaves reveal the last wanderings
of dogs slipped from their yards, the last ball
kicked into the street, and fathers pulling into
driveways, a panorama of privacies funneled
towards family rooms and kitchen tables, the small
admonishments and routines, the static
of belonging to a tribe . . .

The hedge breathes around the child
for whom time slows. Crickets fill the night
with furious courtship, while the last breath
of twilight deepens to thicken the secrecy
of those bushes, the omniscience of being
tribeless, a witness overseeing one's world

like a superhero waiting in secret
to make just the right move, her thoughts
filling a bubble over her head, preparing
one bold act that will set her apart
and fix the future for everyone. Her eyes
behind the leaves take in the panorama
of lawns as though from the sky, before she
too is called into rooms drawn against the barely
grasped, the infinite. And then into bed. All night
the bushes hum with her abandoned solitude,
holding an act still waiting to take shape.

Are there sections? Consider transitions

Consider an absence—space
between dots, no-man's-land dividing
claimed turf, mundane event left
off the page, break in dialogue, intake

of breath, pause before decision—
as volte. A presence. Where something quiet
happens or holds up or is preparation

for the next demand. Not completion.
Not the blank I drew when I first
learned to jump horses, so relieved
to have cleared a fence and stayed
aboard, I forgot for a moment

there was another one ahead.
I forgot to breathe. I stepped away
from myself and then struggled

to regroup, all monkey mind
and indecision as we approached the next
place to leave the ground. The horse
flicked an ear, wondering if I was

still there . . . Thus the difference
between apprentice and master:
seeing the demand between demands.
Showing up inside it.

Turn it upside down

Don't shake it.
    Wait
        for something like
            mica
                moonstone
                    revelation
       to question its contract
                with gravity
         and (re)position itself
             in suspension
               base notes thinned
                        to harmonic threads
              Latin letters
                 loosened from
                    parchment
                       monument
                to drift
          to cave wall
              salt bed
                constellation
     the way weather
       inside a snow globe loosens
                in the hands of a child
        who believes
           in the weightless
              landscape
           (ask-and-it-is-given)
             ready to astonish.

Define an area as "safe" and use it as an anchor

There's a space inside *waiting*
where nothing has to happen.

The mind's machinery
gears down, releasing only a *tick*

now and then, like a heater
turned off. Wheels on stone shake

ground far from here, as
something like egg white beaten to air

holds me the way this morning I held a vole
in down-gloved hands, carrying it

from the cat's jaws back to furrowed earth
and brown grass. It didn't struggle

in that softness, that transport, and even
allowed me to stroke its head briefly

with my thumb, giving all of itself over
to a suspension between

the facts of its life
and a chance to begin again.

You are an engineer

Consider
    sprocket
        ball bearing
            aqueduct
                crane &
                    hook, stalwart
                pulley
        as metaphor
or
    tensile
        canvas fashioned into
                aerodynamic
                    lift & drag
  & flint into
            thermal conduction
  & the wheel into
            dynamic stability
    as poetry—
what keeps
    the skyline
        upright
            & allows it to
    hold layered striations of
        stairways, floors, ductwork, closets, small change,
            footfalls over wood & tile, fridges full of food
            & drink
                in various
                    thermal states?

What   do
        words
                & holes between them
                            & holes words fit
        have to do with
                draft & design?
So hard
        (vital)
                to make utterance into
        durable
                netting
                        or edifice of
                            intricate collaborations

        or vessel
                strong enough to
                        cradle, over
                                troubled
                waves, its own air.

What mistakes did you make last time?

I counted wrong

I used too many abstractions

I missed the exit

I fell off the dock walking backwards in the dark

I mistook the distinguished guest for a waiter

I kept talking after I had made my point

I revved the engine thinking I was in reverse

I made my horse cross the cattle guard

I forgot the quiche was in the oven

I forgot to buckle the top buckle

I said "blackface" while giving a lecture on Berryman's *Dream Songs*

I forgot the emergency brake

I ate salty chips while drinking single malt straight up

I didn't look at my notes

I didn't cut enough

I cut too much

I didn't proofread

I didn't honor my boundaries

I lost my temper

I rushed the ending

Once I sat quietly and waited, empowered
by silence, but forgot to do it again.

Disconnect from desire

Imagine every hunger
swept aside—like this morning,
spring-wet snow having erased
branch, asphalt, sunlight
and cutting the power across
a swathe of county. This morning
our windows frame a world muted
and packed with gauze. A world
sleeping in. No coffeepot.
No internet. The clocks wait.
Nothing to do but light a candle and let
aimlessness flow into it like ink
through a pared nib . . .
Then a flare—a string of notes
catching hold, a phrase
to be followed—and *desire*
has nosed its way
in, because all along
it craved the *disconnect*.

Ghost echoes

Lead crystal holding wine
or water loves the light
press of finger tracing its rim.
At first no sound, then a tensile
hum fills the room as though

waiting all along—clear, otherworldly
hum-blossom rising from the stem no one can see.
It silences dinner chatter, this trick
to pass time between courses,
though the sound, a tactful god, gathered

long before in the glassblower's
breath and blue flame. Now it
lingers, thins, and disperses
like smoke into the light as each hand
flutters back to napkin or fork

and talk resumes. But the silent glass
sings still, a vibration I can feel
through my finger hovering over the fine-
blown rim; so the god of flesh
can rouse the god of glass again.

Left channel, right channel, centre channel

Brian Eno's *Music for Airports* replays
aimlessness. Repetition. The sound of
whole days glassed in and blurred. Synthesized
voices drift from recessed speakers, confined

to three or four notes moving almost
nowhere, each note suspended in its own
reverberation—the way travelers drift
inside the locked space of Security.

Daydream and desire recede in fluorescence
and the endless current of others cut off from
home, destination, recognizable faces—
in airports we turn invisible. To ourselves.

We miss a connection, rebook, and wait while
the mind's music idles. Mechanical failure.
Weather. The world itself delayed or timed out.
No point fighting this current, says the music.

The composer himself has surrendered. Stay
with him. In the middle. And go where it takes you.

Only one element of each kind

A single smudge to skew the Golden Mean.
One B-flat to jolt the key
of C. One charcoal curve, hint at supple
neck flowing into shoulder. Grain
of asphalt or pinch of ash to deepen
the wine. A spill of yellow, mellow pill
to lift one gray dawn, or view of tired
snow through a shard of green
beach glass. One raspberry
out of season. Then another

taste of summer while February
lowers a single sheet of cloud over
the house that darkens fast. A single lamp
to shape the dusk. The singular
shape of frost-flake before warmed air
drips it from windshield. The one life
that ends too soon—how it takes
the whole of a life
to grasp this.

Do we need holes?

This morning's downpour keeps us
grateful inside our cinder block
enclosure and the breath/stretch
space yoga has made
while light outside barely
reaches the wattage of dusk.
All night the sky lowered for this—

now it tears itself apart, deafening
and scary. We breathe
under water, inside this room-
bubble, a hole in the rain.
What did early humans think when
something they couldn't see seemed
to turn itself inside out, when water

rushed like this from a rent sky?
What shelter could trees offer, as rain
drove through holes between
leaves? Was the air itself
on the way to ruin? What else might fall
or swell from holes no one could see?
Even now, knowing better, I burrow

into a cave that opens inside me
and taste the *not-knowing* that must have chafed
mankind into words, into cultivation
and crop, into welcoming rain through holes
in the light, into worshipping rain
as partner to sun, into naming
the earth *mother*.

Honor thy error as hidden intention

Robert Motherwell raised his brush,
muttering, his whole body stretching
into his mistakes. I have uttered

wrong words, clichés
that fell flat but sometimes led
away from themselves to unexpected
freedoms, and misspellings turned visitations—

once I wrote "slightful" and felt a little ghost
tickling my shoulder. See
how spilled toothpicks make a lattice

Mondrian lost and found himself in?
Water everywhere finds its way
down, creating fissures/havoc/mud,
tumbling and buffing river stones

to a smoothness Henry Moore loved
as silhouette and skin, woman, repose—
gravity never apologizes for a mess

though I have made errors from which
the court inside me will *never*
let me off. Fault line, plucked nerve
of shame . . . Jackson Pollock

just poured more paint
on the canvas every time a can—*oops*—
tipped over.

You can only make one dot at a time

Riverbank—
            plane tree—
dappled sun—
                    bustle—
parasol—
                    top hat—
did Seurat envision
                the paraphernalia
of repasts al fresco
when he began
                A Sunday on La Grande Jatte
        with his slimmest
                    brush, making
        each
                dot
                        separate
                        & letting no
                                white show?
                        He must have loved
                the mathematics of
                                patience
        & maybe
                more—one
                        oblique
                                gesture
        in its moment   his eye
                    all depth of field
                                & saturation's
                        duet between
                                absence & presence

                dab & pause—
the viewer's eye
            did
                    still does
                        the rest   yearning
            towards coherence (never mind
                            seasons
                                    fickle light

            fingers cramping on the brush)
        and the illusion
            of having   banished
                            (dwelling between
            the dots, aching in its cradle)
                            time itself.

Look closely at the most embarrassing details and amplify them

1. Your face beaten by sunlight—
breaking the promise of the flawless young clerk
at the Clinique counter—its riverbeds and seared patches.

Try another hour in the sun, no lipstick, your
gray roots untended—somewhere, women
stride wild in their invisibility.

2. Your great-aunt's scalloped silver and chintz.

Add gilt-rimmed goblets, chipped Wedgwood
and fingerbowls passed also from another century.

3. Pigment that refuses to yield like meringue
or icing under your palate knife.

Consider Ivan Albright's Fisherman
painted layer by layer over months,
all corrugation and sandcastle splendor, sea-
darkened face holding light in its tired folds.

4. Smudged ink, watercolor spilling, nothing
recognizable, not even a hint.

After the Great War, action painting
ranked gesture over figure, and colors departed
known territory for hues never named—it offended
everyone, and bathed New York in limelight.

5. Those tremolos and grace notes
where silence, please, would be golden.

Think jazz riff—all motif & variation, self-
hypnosis, spontaneous, call-and-
response, no end in sight, each moment
pushed to limits where silence
doesn't even want to catch its breath.

Is the tuning appropriate?

Attenuated A before the maestro
steps out—the note unfolds, golden wing,
from a single bow stroke to waken
woodwind and brass, gutstring and ivory—
pulling the stream of notes into its furl
where, after ritual dissonance
and waverings, they swirl into one thread,
a timbre redolent of plush and polish—
tasteful—calibrated—marking
a modest release of anticipation.
It's matinee day at Symphony Hall
where most of the regulars are over eighty-five.

Propped by investments, children who visit
when they can, and résuméd caregivers, they
bob over canes and folding walkers,
late to their seats, their skin translucent,
hair thinned to auras, invisible except when
someone impatient wants to pass. Easy
to forget they were once quick, graceful,
eyes clear and backs straight—and beautiful
to someone or many. Some faced bullets and flames,
watched the slaughter of friends and didn't
back down. Some bore heartbreak on their shoulders
until love or hope could find its way again

and again—and what does it mean to
raise a family? To lift and keep it aloft
when resolve wavers, when a middle child
steals from the neighbors or leaves home

and never looks back, when a first spouse
shuts down the future for a time, when savings
are gambled away—what grit, to forgive
and forgive, and then forgive the body
as it fails. Each patron has bathed and dressed
and left safe space for this moment
when the concertmaster offers the first
burnished note of the afternoon. It's matinee day
at Symphony Hall, where most of the regulars
are breakable. May the music treat them gently.

Take away the elements in order of apparent nonimportance

Leave one Russian pianist at a baby grand
to fill the room with Mussorgsky's *Pictures*

at an Exhibition, but take away the paintings
the music reimagines—the massive ox
before its cart that blends with night, chicks
hatching in an orange wash of dawn, the Kiev
gate's mass and scalloped turrets . . .

Take away the pianist's arrival by plane.
Take away the flight he'll take tomorrow

and his nights in hotel beds,
the bottled water, the bows taken
since he was eight.

Take away the score

because the music comes to him
afresh each time he opens the portal
of his body which itself disappears, leaving
the sheen of his brow and cheekbone
as he closes his eyes and surrenders
to the instrument,

and how can we not shrug off
the weight and shame
of being *human* and glimpse
something diamond-pure
for a moment, in ourselves?

Give the game away

The place to begin: blindfolded.

Wait for impulse, tender
animal, to direct you away from

known obstacles and the press
of others' hunger—What *is*

competition, and what would feed you
without it? Pretend

depths of the night
with your friendly familiar. Pretend

a self not braced against what the others
are doing—let all of them win

and then wait. In that fissure that deepens
before dawn, a hole down which

the sleepless mind plummets, the choice
is to drift somewhere you've never been

or be afraid. Bored. Baffled. Try
drift, try free fall without the win

to hold you up, try
the thought that all along there was

nothing to lose.

Use fewer notes

Let an absence expand
    harmony threads,
        space between notes a hammock

for reverie. And words?
        Where might we be
            with breath alone?

Returned to
    senses?
        A lost summer blooms

from midcentury doo-wop
    on Classic Vinyl; first love from
        a vial of Old Spice or Shalimar

years after that heedless
    rush to grow—up? away?—suddenly
        we revisit less encumbered versions of

  self, the promises
    we half kept and then
        forgot, replacing daydream

with modest achievement
    clutter of passwords
        and rechargeable devices designed

to relieve us of suspension, silence,
    the tease of uncertainty, chord or phrase
        that might have left intervals for *what next?*

part **II**

LEFT-HAND TIME

Abandon normal instruments

Sing through a grass blade,
hum under water, draw breath
across the ribs, soak up five seconds
of vibrato through soles of the feet,
let the tiny ear hairs separate
and rework a hesitant riff into surprise
and glitter—who needs the flute's
polished keys, or the baroque
burnished cello with its catgut
moan?—test blade, breath,
and the ground underfoot in registers
never attempted, a chamber blend
of difficult passages working
their way nearly by accident
to perfection. They will make
a theater of you, all chandelier
and red plush—every seat sold out—
no room for the critic
who once kept a box there.

Imagine the music as a chain of disconnected events

Michael Wolff can work
two keyboards at once—one
behind him—without looking—
his left hand feline—nimble
as his right—he doesn't know which hand
does what—it's all cascades—waves
of sound move through him,
acoustic—is his Tourette's
part of the gift?—it puts him on edge—
the small hum at the back of his throat—
Keith Jarrett did it too—lost himself
over the keyboard because losing himself
was the heart—the serrate edge
between control and loss—momentum
and chaos—like Miles Davis's cauldron of
dissonance and driving beat, *Bitches Brew*—
I pour it over ice when I'm ready
to shed obligation—self—residue
of logic—and slip into—
something that fits.

Use an unacceptable color

Puce.
Chartreuse.
Magenta the shade of
raw beef left in the sun.
The auroras *borealis* and *australis*
seething with combustion,
carried into mankind's sliver
of sight by solar wind

that riles oxygen atoms into
plasma—*magnetospheric*—
violet, red, bruise blue, iterations
of green—photographs reveal
improbable neon curtains, streamers,
rays, fire over ice, earth and sun fusing
their atmospheres in a wash of charged
particles that crest into *chorus wave*
over polar caps where few humans
dwell, huddled against relentless white.

Astronomers say yellow-green
is the most common.
Color of sickness in the liver.
Color that suits few complexions.
Color to get out of bed for
in regions where the sun barely
peers over the horizon in midwinter—
miracle one could pass a hand
through, if one could reach into
such unthinkable solitude.

Make an exhaustive list of everything you might do and do the last thing on the list

Cut the modifiers.
Cut the sugar and
ease up on salt.
Extend the metaphor.
Take something out.
Add something
out of the blue—a clear
winter sky, a heron levitating
from thready reeds . . . Banish
all similes but one. Check
your inbox. Disturb
the line breaks. Change
the title. Ditch punctuation.

Save the fourth line for later.
Violate the margins.
Add lemons, toothpaste
and olives. Replace
two predictable words.
Say the opposite of
what you planned
to say (but never say
yes unless you mean it).
End three lines earlier.
Begin one stanza later.
Go out for a run
with someone else's poem.

Fall in love.

Twist the spine

. . . how the cat
    slides upside down
        from a lap and
            lands right-side-
        soundless; slides
    as though his bones were
made of river;
    how the river; how
        the young tree
            (how the wind
        pauses to let it
    straighten); how
the breath; how the parched
        arroyos; how the used
        body; how
tendon and surrender;
    how translucence flows
        over muscle as two skewed
    vertebrae align
        like a sentence finally
            completing
        itself . . .

Into the impossible

Think *sky*—realm
of no resistance to another

countdown to risk, chance, the next question
and the next—how else

did all we now take for granted
come to be? Flame, flint, airborne arrow,

hard-boiled egg, penicillin, combustion,
the bowling pinsetter, microchip, Velcro,

laser needle unerring in its pierce
and seal, all born from space

grand enough to hold failures
and accidents, draft after draft, the *why*

not? the *what if?* the *nothing
to lose*, the zone, the pushed

envelope, Hail Mary, bungee jump, brass
ring, lure cast into shadow, the luck, the leap

through error—
then the landing.

Accept advice

from unexpected sources—not
the stonemason's crowning
cathedral, but his long apprenticeship
and the beautiful failures of his youth.
The way his hands knew the tools.
The way he saw through stone to fault line.
Perhaps his sons never joined him
in the guild, perhaps the cathedral fell
accomplice to corruption, perhaps
you're wondering what any of this
has to do with advice. Try
coming at it sideways.

Simple subtraction

peel away   head noise
    each layer reveals another strident layer
               underneath
                  the obvious   what do you have
   to lose?
       (self-regard/income/reason for getting up)
so much static   no wonder you can't
    write/sing/set brush
          to whiteness (canvas)
             chalk to roughness (asphalt)

    hear
       a few
           green notes
      in midsummer/monsoon/high-desert
        afternoons that might lead to chord
       or fugue or amazingly tall
         snapdragons/dahlias
              spilling from pots
           in spite of you
don't we all want
      one solid
         night's sleep
   to clear out   doubt/regret   and set us at first light
  four-cornered   toes spread
    to meet earth's *I've got you?*
    not to mention the sun's
      and the moon's
         I'm yours in darkness and in light
     and stars that sequin deep space
           light-years after
     their light is gone

Mechanicalize something idiosyncratic

The Moog synthesizer rendered Bach
at speeds no human hand could
match. Mortal flesh flipped switches,
turned knobs and pressed something
like pedals but not, guiding voltage
through tangled circuitry to transistor
tubes and voila!—clavichord resurrected,
each note an ice chip inside its split
second, even as its clones gathered
and looped to fugue, propelling
Brandenburg to the top of the charts.

Then the nonmusic—New Age, psychedelics,
otherworldly vowels from the Other Side—
Crimson & Clover dismantled the human voice,
squeezing it through a strainer to an infinity
of echoes, slipping electronic composition
into AM radio before Pink Floyd
drenched it in discordant renditions of
one bad trip after another. *Abbey Road*
threaded Lennon's hushed voice blends
through electronic bass, easing
the gap between musician and machine

and Mannheim Steamroller's *Fresh Aire*
transposed epic to melody, melody to
ambiance—an entire album freshened
Odysseus's wanderings—fusing pneumatic
synthesizer with harpsichord, pipe organ,
flute, violin—and by then, where *was*

the line between composer and engineer—
real and programmed fantasy/perception—
chords of the past and harmonics
of the future? And when, lured
closer, did we stop asking?

Consult other sources:
promising, unpromising

Not thought. Perhaps
root—blind, insistent. Not
articulate. A mother's
body contracts,
labors, and the infant
surrenders—that kind of
force. Not elegant. Essential
and focused.

Or breath. Not
visible. Likewise, not
articulate. It lifts
and scours and moves
thought that is no-thought
through the driven
mind, smoothing
tumbled sheets and polishing
the view through
a different window.

Or silence. How
John Cage made music
out of nonsound, only to
discover sound
is never absent. How it
pleased him (when it pleased
no one) to welcome
a world for which
no room had been made.

Ask people to work against their better judgment

Go ahead—*fling* yourself against it.
As in: take away the net; thrum
with vertigo; surprise yourself in dark
glasses and brimmed hat pulled low,
so exotic you might find yourself
asking for an autograph. As in: slip
from the conference room and not tell
yourself where you're going—

out of the neighborhood and all
the dependable gridlocks. Into a realm
that simmers beneath the topography
of your thoughts. Beyond the language
that has served you like a slipper
and the careful walls that kept out
rains fragrant with dirt and damp leaves . . .
You may not see yourself again

but watch for someone
vaguely familiar, still
in transit, fumbling
a new tongue into hand signals
and hybrid phrases, fingers
alive with something about to
be said perhaps
for the first time.

Accretion

The way layer upon layer of
camber builds over tree trunk
or calcium over living bone
while some brain cells, honed
to instinct by a history of mishaps, may
increase. *Launch many expendable efforts*
said William Stafford, loved mentor
and maker of poems. He meant
opt for frequency of attempt. And trust
that something unassailable will evolve
the way runoff and tectonic shifts
made eons of microscopic inroads below
earth's surface before a single mountain
made itself known.

Don't be frightened to display your talents

A single guitar
and a small pot of fire
on a Paris stage: Angelo Debarre,
in wing tips and a fedora that's been around,
his fingers a blur over strings, and I'm in a Roma camp
outside Marseille. Before the War. Firelight
and gold dancing in a tin cup. Manouche.

One by one, others surface
from the shadows—bass, clarinet,
accordion, violin—the music hasn't two
francs to rub together and later will sleep
under the stars. The music nods to each man as he
passes his solo on, honoring another comrade's
long apprenticeship—any one of them
could hold the stage alone, fingers sparked
with wind and experiment. Wave after wave,

the music feeds the fire, the music fills
the stage that is no longer a stage, this music
believed to steal children, that ties its black
hair in a red kerchief and clicks its heels,
music of gaunt cheek and fine bone, Django
and jazz, the lament of flamenco, chrome
and ivory, catgut and breath—it flashes its gold tooth
through the Romany night. The tamped lightning
strikes and strikes.

Repetition is a form of change

and change
        a sly iteration
            of repetition
weather circles us
          solstice to solstice—by calendar
     repeats itself   by jet stream
                 plays fickle

Mid-May   hard frost
             snow returns
   across longitudes
        to shred blossoms
      behind the house
    last year's apples   a memory
           nestled in vanished green
this year stillbirthed
      in frost's pewter grip
           what will be left?

Ghost sweetness   frost-seared leaves
        chafing against each other while magpies
   quarrel   molting for summer   one feather
drops   echo of bird heart
       & warm air cushioned
   between chilled night and bird body

Soon evenings   will linger
     Like   midlife
        expected weather
   softening the way dew

                    passes the night
This morning   pewter sheen
              a meadowlark sings
                  gold filigree
                        persistence
                          on a thin chain

A line has two sides

If you let your eyes lose focus, even
cross, as you stare at that line,

soon you find yourself seeing from a soft
third eye, one you didn't know

was there, and the line's two sides blur
to three. It's like teasing apart

then reuniting voices of rain all night while drifting
in and out of sleep: bouts of wind

and soft drops that rustle leaves, then
torrent noise that fills the open window

as a gutter overflows, drowning out
what so gently began. But the three sounds

remain, rushing and subsiding,
inviting you to listen for the ones

you can't hear or didn't hear at first. And you can
do this all night, through the one ear

not buried in the pillow,
then both at once.

Change instrument roles

Let an oboe take the part
of first violin in a chamber group
of strings—breath pressed through
reed harvested from marshland, oddly
a stringed sound that weaves among
the clear notes pulled by rosined
horsehair over gut strung taut;

so the trumpet turns brass into air
and light—or something like light—
muting its glare to mesh with the caramel
tones of the opera star whose throat
trembles with effort. Both collaborations
offer depths of fertile marsh.
Both move with the grace of a cat

leaping to a single uncluttered spot.
Both weave caramel into gold
like dawn breaking over birds that awaken
all at once and layer the air
with song while the cat crouches
below, all pinnacle and purpose
in his native element, ready to leap

for the thrill of it, not for the kill.

Lowest common denominator check:
single beat, single note, single riff

Step-on-a-crack sets the beat,
    the stress-tap-step
urging lilt and continuance—why
    can't chance
        carry the next note
           and the next, each note unplanned
    and solid when it comes?
Another square to step on, another
    crack to leap, a mother's back to keep
        intact, another beat
           to quell the mind's redundancies—who needs
           words? Who needs
        connections?
One note repeats itself
    calling off the guards within, calling in
        purpose and drum-trance-
           stress-step lilt and leap,
                no bone breaking
but daring to dance something new into
    the same old walk to school
        and home again, free-
           wheeling from the blackboard room.

Make a blank valuable by putting it in an exquisite frame

Or make the blank
the frame where words
aren't—the vertical silence
inside which each slender
cluster of words ends
in temporary
suspension, catapult
driving eye and ear,
through accelerated
current, into a finished
thought. For a moment.
But best is the tease
of almost-meaning within
each margin, line
by line—the flash
that holds
before it empties
into deeper
surprise, a nugget
of sense, prismatic
chip of thought inside
that frame of no-words
that has forced
a pause. This
is the rigor of the line
break, coaxing the flow
of attention just so—
through the (exquisite)
aqueduct of the blank.

Cascades

Noun
for silvery—
unhurried, drifting
downward in
sunlight. Or frothed
with purpose, tumbling
over rocks from a height.

Verb
for scallop shape
multiplying, crescent or
corkscrew in motion, damp
hair feathering over skin over
vertebrae, residual curl and, right
there, ember, a lover's touch

remembered.

Use an old idea

A scrap—
    discard,
        glittery patch seam-ripped
            from a forgotten
                passion
    or dream fragment waiting
        in a swathe
          of night flannel
  or a worn-at-the-elbows argument—
           its remnant of sturdy weave—
use them all, the outgrown
        overlooked
           unfinished, each
      thought-swatch
        freed
  to refresh its colors
        alongside new neighbors—
no lonely sleeve
      no torn hem
          no near revelation
        wasted.

Is it finished?

Is it honest?
Is it the right kind of raw?
Does it please?
Does it provoke?
Does it begin too early?
Need to lose weight?
        Carry itself far from its beginning
                without
                      breaking the thread?
Is it brave?

Does it need more red?
        Less you?
           A tuck? A trim?
                A diagonal hemline?
Do the amethyst and citrine play well together?
                Quartz and peridot?
                      Garnet and turquoise?
Does it need more bass?
        More oboe?
           Unlikely strains of mandolin?

Is the line between
        night sea and night sky
                soft enough?

Does it invite?
Is it patient?
        Curious?
           Does it have a sense of humor?

Does it make a silk purse out of what it doesn't know?

Did the work set you into yourself?
Free you?
Make you cry?

Did you feel your sap rise?

part III
BACK-BEAT TIME

Do nothing for as long as possible

I stare at the keyboard and find myself
drifting to the construction site nearby—
jackhammers and drills in layered
symphonics, excavators dumping soil
from prehistoric jaws, crane releasing a stream
of cement that must be directed quick
while it's wet, rapid-fire Spanish as workers
spread foundation and lay pipe—it's a noisy
mess out there. A work of engineering
whose grid work will yield a high-
end market lit softly with track lights, heat
and refrigeration purring through ducts, shelves
stocked with shine and color, a cornucopia
unimaginable to most of the world.
These men know circuit and sewer.
Leverage and switch. The gears of costly
mammoths that dig and dump and lift.
If our cities were razed, lands stripped
and food made scarce, they'd be
the new elite. Tonight they will wash
another day of labor from their bodies
and sit down to dinner without wondering,
as I do most of the time while hours slip
seamlessly as though through vents
going who knows where, what it means
to have done enough.

Faced with a choice, do both

I wish I was dead
a friend mumbled on the chairlift a month
after his wife died, mumbled so low
I wasn't sure I heard, after I
asked how he planned to spend
his winter. *Dead* his voice, the sear
cauterized small talk, his abyss
now mine. I had never heard this
in a voice before—utterance from the realm
of endings. I touched his arm, feeling
the chill slice me, bind me, and then
we skied down that sparkling mountain,
dead, dead, as we carved our turns
from the habit of living, *dead* a curtain
I suddenly could not part, vacuum I could
never again dismiss, *dead* the two of us
savoring our skills even then because
what else could we do as our skis
caressed from memory the loved
terrain and bright snow, sunlight
touching us *dying* all over.

Give way to your worst impulse

The low-grade fever
was permission, my one task
to mend, my companion the body
asking for soup, a little reading, a half page
of scribbling, hot tea, an apple cut
into eighths. Three days absent of
errand, seamless and quiet, my strings
cut from the strenuous world—I was
free to float. I stared at glints of
quartz in a handful of sunlit stones
and at dust motes making fractals
in air I had never thought a *presence*.

The cat approved, seeing in me
a co-conspirator of doze and drift, sharing
every shifting patch of sun. I savored
Sex in the City reruns and microwave popcorn
long past its sell date. I read anything I wanted,
put it down when I wanted, and napped
whenever drowsiness tempted me
further into the delicious murk. Each hour
held me, expanding gently to hold random
thoughts. I sketched the first in a suite of
poems questioning the disciplined mind
that assumes itself the one fine tool.

Spectrum analysis

The brain toys with *spectrum*. And resists
analysis. It wants to play in the underground
walkway between United terminals B and C
at O'Hare, whose architect designed a quarter mile
of fluorescent tubes overhead in a breathless progression
of hues—washed sky to aqua to cobalt, blush
to crimson to purple, russet paling to shades
of sunrise, an entire rainforest of greens . . .
Slow down, brain. Try again.
Why did Brian Eno think *spectrum* or *analysis* might
get composers out of a rut? His chords morph so slowly
from register to register, they could be lava settling
to landmass. To sand. Water repeating itself
for eons over rock to carve a canyon. *Eno. Eon.*
When he got stuck he stayed right where he was
until he wasn't. Modern physics? There's proof
that time slows at ground level, and stops
inside the event horizon, though
only neutrinos can get there . . .
Eno settled for repeat, repeat, repeat
until nuance finally broke free and fed
a tiny shift in the ambient hush of his music
which, piped over airport speakers, reinforces
the glassy state of patrons in transit—
unlike my neon tunnel that distracts
the jaded traveler from where he's been
and where he's going, and leaves him
trying to choose which fleeting
color he likes best.

The inconsistency principle

Consider the *flying buttress*:
      airborne   stationary
    space-mass hybrid
        in stone
  half-wing
    that doesn't displace
        air
      but launches from its
          massive pier a lateral thrust
  against tonnage   quarried   stacked
            & carved for centuries into
      transept   nave   apse
          saints &
      angels meticulously
        wrought in their musculature and
        robes
     gargoyles leering from parapets
        and the parapets themselves
        heavy
          lacework seen from the
          ground—
it eased vast medieval
    crypt space that needed
      windows
        to interrupt
    intractable walls
        and let in the light of the world
      i.e.
        the Divine

i.e.

relief & transcendence

from & to

load-bearing stone

and did so by pushing it sideways.

Listen to the quiet voice

It rises from
bedrock and flows free

of sediment, the debris of abandoned lots,
free of toxins—you can

drink it. You can see
through it. You can hold it

to your window as prism, ambered
glass over glass through which

the tattered neighborhood
pulls itself together.

You can wear it—think *scarf*—
spun breath at your neck singing

softly with other colors you've put on
and leaving you vivid in the tired streets

where weeds, fresh shards of green, press
through cement to drink the light.

Fill every beat with something

Each time I face the *nothing*
of the not-yet made, of aimless thinking
before a *thought*, I type words
one by one into the silence as though
threading gemstones on a string—
lapis, jade, jasper, turquoise—
for the pleasure of juxtaposition free
of meaning. Stones need only light
to ignite them, translucent
conversing with opaque, earth tones
and mined brilliance exchanging saturations.

In the Garden: a world without
speech, birdcalls lacing
the dawn, the silvery swish of mice
moving through fern, sun throwing into relief
citrine and crimson fruit among leaves overhead.
Today: silence of first snow filled
with pearl and slate, wind blowing shards
of lowered sky, moisture shifting against itself.
The silence melted into my socks
and pinched my nose. My teeth ached.

When I came in, I heard the vents
breathing. I heard my blood return
to my fingers. A lamp tumbled sunstone
through smoke-quartz dusk as the house
flared around me.

What would your closest friend do?

She would tuck a silk scarf behind her belt and pretend she was a horse

She would be the one kid who used a fountain pen

She would keep a Venus flytrap in her bedroom window

She would trade dog tags with the shyest boy in middle school

She would straighten her hair

She would go to the prom with the class nerd

She would write papers ahead of deadline so she could go to forgettable frat parties

She would steer clear of whisky mixed with anything sweet

She would deflect mentors' advances by feigning ignorance

She would leave New York so she could write about New York

She would spend hours crafting elliptical, visionary poems despite her spouse being the recognized writer

She would switch to painting once her poems became famous

She would meditate while the family quarreled

She would listen to anything her kids had to say

She would guard her best friend's worst secret

She would return to poems once her paintings became famous

She would let her perennials spill beyond their plot

She would let her hair go its own way

Infinitesimal gradations

How did Turner nudge pencil sketch to
wash of blended oils to moonlight
filtered through a scrim of cloud?

How did he move from
architectural edge and precision

to nimbus, speed, suggestion—the early
steam engine a blur thrusting itself
through the English mist

or a ship tossed between froth and sky?
He left a legacy of slow dissolves
without evidence of daub or bristle, as though

no coarse body, bearing its feuds and failings
and telltale Cockney accent, wielded the brush.

As though light breathed like thought over
landscapes seen from a height, turrets washed
in sunrise, the parting of Hero and Leander

barely emerging from the densities
of time, a ship on the verge of its wreck
prefiguring its own disappearance

as the artist himself disappeared,
leaving suggestions of wholeness emerging

from proffered parts—like the full ghost-moon

that sometimes swells, shadow-soft
behind the new sliver of moon on a clear night—

a fullness so see-through, so maybe-not-
there, we wonder if we pieced it ourselves
from a fragment of vanished light.

Don't be afraid of things because they're easy to do

Shame the bass note,
the drumbeat, *shame* the Puritan
mandate to sweat and suffer,
shame the thought that comes
without effort (small
and ripe for cliché),
shame to turn from paid
work and feel a quiet lift
while filling the bowl with torn
lettuce, *shame* to feel a return
of well-being while digging weeds
from the bed of catmint,
shame the calm dirt humming
as cleared roots make room for worms
to do their invisible work, *shame*
to aerate the mind with the hand
that digs down to moisture.

Use filters

Some sere
winter days, the sky's
palette of clouds spreads
layered densities to soften
ridge and tree line and erase,
in a gradual wash, Kachina's
implacable dome—then
for a moment it allows
veiled sun to bleed through
as nimbus, spectrum, halo
of muted rays mixed with snow squalls,
a gift—otherworldly for being
temporary—as though God
Herself had left harsher labors
to flick a pale gold brush
over the leaden season,
inviting us to look down less
and behold?—receive?—the hues of
unexpected kindness.

Humanize something free of error

This morning is error-
fraught—eight inches of snow
spring-wet, cement
on the shovel that makes
no dent in the driveway
that stretches, endless,
power lines above it crusted
and shut down. And the town?—
even the plows can't
cut through.

A roaring—wind
or thunder?—March
on this mountain is lion-lamb-
lion, all caprice and surprise,
the power flicking back on
just long enough to remind us
how helpless we are. Nothing

to soften the din outside,
the clash of winter and
equinox. My workplace is closed
until further notice and the morning
expands, promising, the weather
a picaresque hero fanning
his winning hand—all the earth's
humors—in a novel I suddenly
have time to linger over.

Get your neck massaged

You think a hot bath or light novel
might do the trick when you're too tired
to meet one more deadline or be nice to anyone,
but you've forgotten about the fine-tuned
sinews and tendons just below the head, bearing
the weight of skull and world of thought
every day, sixteen hours, just as the arch
of each foot holds the universe of the body as you
load it and let it carry you, never caressing it
in thanks. And still, your breakthrough
notions, most efficient moves, happen when
fatigue overrides the will and the need for praise,
some part of body stepping in to finish the work
without the rest of you. So thank the neck,
faithful Atlas—allow it the press of warm hands
scented with oil until it gives up its ghosts
and cracks the locks behind which exhaustion
has confined itself to twinges you've grown used to—
let it release trapped sorrows to clouds
of touch by a seer whose hands can read
the troubled braille beneath your nape. Then
let those hands work their way down.

Look at a very small object, look at its centre

Centre. Not
center—not *middle*
but *through.* A passage
to overlooked worlds—the pebble
packed with a history
of forms—mountain
thrust up by fire, ground by ice
to sand, and repacked. Quark-sized
chips of light held in small surround—
as in opal, sunstone, lapis with
pinprick galaxies of gold, granite
pocked with mica . . . And when your
house cat blinks awake in a patch
of winter sun, her pupils black dots
in depths of gold, you may see
ibex streaking across a savannah
in the carrion light of sunset,
rainforest canopy jeweled with macaw
and glints of snake, a lineage
so much longer than ours—
of tiger stripe, leopard splash,
and deft recline along primordial
branch. Her tufted ear
still tilts to this.

Think of the radio

... for example, the blond-wood console
where your grandparents gathered, a map
of Europe before them as they traced Hitler's
shadow spreading through France, while Roosevelt

from his fireside sought to calm them—
and in London night after night, deep underground
through blackouts and strafings, the BBC
kept lit the candle of King's English.

•

... and the hive on your first nightstand—
built of something like Bakelite, frame
and crosspieces trussing its speakers
like chrome on a midcentury Chevy—

it eased you away from the Void, *Dragnet*
breathing beside your pillow, its music
scarier than its plots but less scary
than your solitude. Later, Wolf Man's

nicotine rasp, the voice of night itself,
introduced you to rock 'n' roll that would
follow you through your teens
on a pink transistor, to the beach

and paneled dens, its single antenna
funneling the swoon of cheek to cheek,
trippy lights, and revved engines—
your future. Hovering.

•

. . . and today's evangelical stations, all
you can pick up while driving late
through lunar stretches of this country if you
don't have satellite—by reflex you reach

to turn them off—but sometimes a familiar
child, peering into the bottomless hour,
reappears inside you, hungry for any voice
that might talk her down from the dark.

Water

In the syntax of surrender

words push gently. Through
doubt, along cracked riverbeds
towards faith, over memory shards
that pierce and pierce until they
don't, buffed by continual motion
of heartbreak and insight stroking,
stroking, and moving on, the sentence
never finished, always changing.

Surrender is fed

by gravity. It invites
improvisation. Soft defiance
of blockage. *Down* is a force, a source
of release, although dams, aggressively
engineered and financed, work
against this—what's held inside
is trapped. And harbors a plan
for spectacular escape.

Surrender en route

is river. Carving, polishing,
digging, asking, more elastic
than the banks that direct it
and more persistent than armature,
bombast, the will's propensity
for feints and jabs.

Surrender's destination

is bowl. It collects all that consents to
flow into stillness even when roiled
by wind. Every sea and lake, every
word tempered by silence, fills
a hollow of its making
and is held.

Mute and continue

Into my fifties
I took for granted the din,
the ravenous voices, waves of
stop and *go*, a constant invention of self
beyond its past, a moon-self waxing
to crack the horizon.

Our forebears lived by din
and rarely lived past it. Hardwired
to plant, build, kill strangers, mend with
herbs, map oceans and leave offspring
as evidence, most passed from the world
midstride, never facing
this quiet, this soft
surround, as another
frontier.

I watch my descendants
forge onward, in hot pursuit
of themselves—irrepressible even
when weary—shedding their skins, rising
and rising from imagined ash—
and remember well the not-enough-
time, the clamor of white noise,
the itch—so I forgive them
their neglect in returning my calls

while small countries that once
received me have vanished
or been overrun, and my passport

seems to have expired, leaving me
spacious. My thoughts cherish
their old habits of itch and reach
but they seem to have lost interest in *me*—
like second-stage missiles, they
use me to soar beyond me.

Emphasize differences

Drum speaks thunder
and hobnail on stone; violin
speaks breeze, bird trill, and trellis;
flute, snowmelt and silver; clarinet,
ebony; French horn speaks brandy and red
livery; trombone, early autumn sun
if it's not too loud, not bonfire set by small boys.
Oboe knows all the animal tongues, and tuba
the tongues of the old country—anyone's old country—
beer keg and packed dirt, boots thumping,
joyful and a little drunk. When this gathering
listens, when the maestro leads it
in listening, when all of them listen
through the composer's ear that heard a single
layered voice rising from inked notes
even after he lost his hearing, they make
a superior voice of voices,
a persuasion that exerts no force
but fills the warrior with kindness, the despot
with self-forgetfulness, the poor with abundance,
the world with a reason to save itself.

Consider different fading systems

(Sheltering, 2020)

Absence of ink on April's calendar.
Of spontaneous errand. Just
this mild swirl of thought—

feather-voice—harbored
by contagion and the stalled
future—my ghost

companion. No need to dress.

Through cell tower and divided
screens, real conversation
is cushioned by familiar lamplight

and Moroccan pillows. On my lap
the cat's drowse, her privacy, melt
into mine. I forget what day it is

while fields across this road
begin to dress for spring
as do the mountains nearby, reaching

into air still safe to breathe.

I take my limbs and imperiled lungs
into them and do not speak
to the others tasting their own dram

of risk and sunlight—a wave, a smile
through the eyes. Nothing leaves
our mouths, all of us masked.

Draped carefully over our bones.

This language of the body
feeds on silence, holding space
while nothing comes to fill it—

no plans, accolades, expectations—
like rooms cleared after
someone has died.

I sleep better. I want to think

something green below the remnants
rests too—fisted, not ready to loosen in its bulb.
The ghost voice breathes *wait, float* over

what is no longer asked of me.

Work at a different speed

You could *go* as O'Hara says
on your nerve—compose
as though chased by thugs—launch
yourself into unfamiliar neighborhoods
without a plan. Welcome unexpected
collisions. Lose your way and then
find it outside your bandwidth,
beyond the used-up signals.

•

Or wander outside. Pull weeds.
Pump the bike tires. Cut up
a melon. Soak the orchid—
how about a fistful
of trail mix or
cup of tea?—let the piece
sneak up & finish
itself. No one has to
know how fraught
with procrastination, how
incremental is the work
of *not* working. Yesterday
I beheld, marveling, a rock-
strewn slash of moraine
as finished sculpture
amid a stand of spruces,
not the glacier
that melted it there.

•

Or wait.

Be cathedral space.

Keep two doors open, one
for in and one for out.

Out is the crucial door.

A small something not-you
will stay. Make an altar (this

was never about pace).

Acknowledgments

I am grateful to the following journals in which some of these poems first appeared:

Catamaran: "Use an unacceptable color"

Cloudbank: "Go slowly all the way around the outside," "Use fewer notes," "Make a blank valuable by putting it in an exquisite frame," "Water," and "Mechanicalize something idiosyncratic"

Nine Mile Magazine: "Honor they error as hidden intention, "Faced with a choice, do both," and "Think of the radio"

Numéro Cinq: "Ask people to work against their better judgment," "A line has two sides," and "Are there sections? Consider transitions"

On the Seawall: "Define an area as 'safe' and use it as anchor," "What mistakes did you make last time?," "Water," and "Consider different fading systems"

Poet Lore: "Abandon normal Instruments," "Accept advice," and "Accretion"

South Florida Poetry Journal: "Is the tuning appropriate?" and "Do nothing for as long as possible"

Thank you also to many readers who have seen these poems and in some cases this manuscript through their many stages: Karen Kevorkian, Jean Nordhaus, Veronica Golos, Cathy Strisik, Judith Thomson, Joan Ryan, Dale Kushner, Betsy Sholl, Andrea Watson, and Rush Rankin.

And special thanks to Hilda Raz and Elise McHugh at the University of New Mexico Press for their ongoing support of my work and for shepherding this book through the grid of acceptance through production.

Unruly Tree